# THE BACKSLIDER

## (LOST SOUL)

## SUPRIYA SINGH

*for ME ;*

*and for everyone relating*

*to IT.*

# Contents

# Contents

# Contents

# Contents

# Contents

# Contents

# Contents

# Chapter1

*She is a verse of emotions*

*which are graved inside her .*

*Showing everything is allright seems*

*so difficult and full of toxicity.*

# Chapter2

*she owns her own perspective to*

*see around and analyze ,*

*it's enough to define herself .*

*Isn't it ?*

# Chapter3

*An average girl with*

*blooming wings to fly*

*at the highest ;*

*thinking further ,*

*will she be able to ?*

# Chapter4

*she observes ,*

*she notices ,*

*but yet she does not*

*complain about it to others.*

*it's just because she considers herself*

*a kind of PHILOSOPHER*

*or maybe because she is too*

*matured of her age.*

# Chapter5

*tears rolled out ;*

*let it go off .*

*it's better .*

*believe it .*

# Chapter6

*people all around but*

*yet refers to the moon .*

*scaring of those who didn't even blew ,*

*shoulders to cry on but*

*pillows are best .*

*to whom on rely to everyone seems to FAKE .*

# Chapter7

*they say : don't overthink .*

*may I ask them , 'then where should I*

*dump down those mixed thoughts & feelings*

*which are abruptly howling in my mind ?'*

# Chapter8

*simple is beautiful ;*

*tending to turn it interesting ,*

*it lost it's beauty in simplicity*

*leaving the things COMPLICATED .*

# Chapter9

*it's good to find a way to*

*express yourself;*

*it's better .*

*But it becomes frustrating*

*when you are not able to that*

*at times .*

# Chapter10

*who says , love happens only once ?*

*every other second we fall in love*

*with things , moments , places , people*

*but that one is special somewhere .*

# Chapter 11

*soul IMPALES*

*but you are ALIVE*

*for you BREATHE .*

*- it's magical*

# Chapter 12

listening most of the times from them:


she can't do anything,


she doesn't know to handle the things,


she blunders.


she is a blunder.


- a secret:

*universe knows her better than anyone else.*

# Chapter 13

*she is the one who loves to write,*

*but hates to speak.*

*she is the one who love silence,*

*but dies without music.*

# Chapter14

*her eyes sees hustle of the city,*

*but somewhere she witnesses*

*a kind of silence in it*

*and she is the one who adores the silence.*

# Chapter15

*sometimes they say :*


*'why she is always so serious?'*


*but they did not notice*


*her cheerful childish side.*


*- it happens*

# Chapter16

*she tries,*

*she tries to find happiness*

*in little things.*

*she actually tries...*

# Chapter17

*yawning after nine hours of sleep,*

*screwing up all,*

*she is confused where she messed up*

*and the things go on...*

# Chapter18

overthinking screws up all.


she witnesses it


each and single time


yet she does it.

# Chapter19

*roses with thorns ,*

*taj mahal with it's hole ,*

*she with her silence .*

*- beautiful with mysteries*

# Chapter20

*she tries to be actual her*

*but the situations and certain environment*

*around her*

*don't allow her to be.*

# Chapter21

*is it necessary ?*

*to have the reasons for everything,*

*can't some of them just be ?*

*is it necessary to have a specific reason*

*all the time ??*

# Chapter22

*a thing which is messed up*

*and messes up the things ??*

*- SHE*

# Chapter23

sometimes , you have to be hard

on yourself ,

you have to make certain decisions ,

it's hurting .

- (you know)

# Chapter24

*it's not easy to let*

*go off the things*

*sometimes...*

*- it's not at all*

# Chapter25

*the best thing carries*

*sorrows , sadness*

*and all of that*

*which makes it*

**THE BEST.**

*- don't run away from sadness;*

*it can be creative.*

# Chapter26

some or the other thing is bothering her,

but what it is, she is unaware of;

she is feeling something,

but what she is unaware of;

juggling to find out at times;

she says to herself,

'let it be, at last everything will be fine.'

# Chapter27

she likes the nightrides,

feeling the calming notes of music

which reaches to her heart,

that cool breeze touches her soul

and her open hair fluttering in the air

reminds her of the bird she

ever wanted to become.

# Chapter28

*a full storm resides in her,*

*but yet she whispers to the flowers...*

*- it's her diversity*

# Chapter29

a full moon in the dark sky ,

it's beautiful to witness

and then there are stars

embracing it's beauty...

# Chapter30

*fears let you become*


*insane, inferior , introvert.*


*maybe she too had...*

# Chapter 31

*hundreds of good deeds is*

*equivalent to one mistake and*

*hundreds of deeds are vanished*

*like the vapours from camphor.*

# Chapter32

*smiling seems quite easy ,*

*but*

*being happy is something different...*

# Chapter33

*somewhere or the other,*

*a phase comes where no one is there*

*by your side;*

*not even your family at times.*

*going through this is the strongest version of
yourself,*

*be proud of IT;*

*be proud of YOURSELF.*

# Chapter34

cuts were there all over her body

such that they were red and swollen

yet not a single tear rolled down her cheeks;

it's there she learnt to swallow the PAIN.

- she met with an accident

# Chapter35

*everyone expects from her to be there*

*on their side and to understand them*

*but who did to her ??*

*she stopped explaining .*

*she stopped expecting .*

*- she feels better now*

# Chapter 36

*the stones were there to stand still,*

*even if you don't know how ?*

*it's somewhere we disrecognise*

*to maker as a faller...*

# Chapter37

*sometimes it seems as she is out of this world,*

*carefree, consequences don't matter,*

*enjoys on her own and carrying herself
unwittingly*

*as if she owns the world without any effort.*

# Chapter38

*her problem is that*

*she thinks too much that with logic sometimes.*

*she knew her problem*

*yet she didn't stop there.*

# Chapter39

'*I am happy in my life*'

*this one is quite rare.*

# Chapter40

out of the track,

somewhere bare,

somewhere fare,

where you want to be;

can be a DARE.

except it to be somewhere

for it actually takes you

*where you care.*

# Chapter41

*DEATH defines how*

*GOOD the being was.*

# Chapter42

*she adopted the habitat,*

*she had around her everyday,*

*it's somewhere she learnt*

*to adjust and compromise.*

# Chapter43

*she can be clear with every aspects of*

*her life;*

*it's bout the segments and*

*this is where she is messed up*

*within herself.*

# Chapter44

*sometimes her silence speaks more than her words*

*and it's hard to hide*

*your eyes from everyone*

*when it is filled with unsaid words.*

# Chapter45

*she arose within herself*

*to be at somewhere ;*

*maybe she can reach there*

*where she unknowingly desires.*

# Chapter46

*she on her own*

*behave sometimes like articulate;*

*and so her*

*unspoken words felt like...*

# Chapter47

*she believes :*

*the worst endings can be the*

*most beautiful beginnings*

*sometimes.*

# Chapter48

*her voice sometimes;*

*acts as invulnerable*

*thought she can be too...*

# Chapter 49

*she is not holding onto old feelings;*


*she just haven't found any new ones yet...*

# Chapter50

*she is severly diagnosed of the*

*symptoms of*

*LISZTOMANIA.*

# Chapter51

she feels comfortable in


darkness of the night.


what she says would sum up


between her and the m

# Chapter52

how far she will go

for the love ;

only she knows...

# Chapter53

*the stars witnesses*

*her flying,*

*leaving behind limitations,*

*beyondness, insecurities, fear...*

# Chapter54

*she is not the WRITER,*


*she witnesses, she observes,*


*she feels*


*and she pens down.*

# Chapter55

*feels though,*

*she is the cause of everything.*

*she tries to avoid it*

*but is used to listen it*

*after a while of couple days...*

# Chapter56

*she is somewhere*

*WEIRDO;*

*which acts as*

*ORDINARY.*

# Chapter57

*she listens to both of them,*

*she understands to both of them*

*but who does to her ??*

# Chapter58

*it's 7:30 p.m,*

*it went DARK*

*and then RAINED and*

*RAINED and*

*RAINED!!*

# Chapter59

*she can't exactly describe*

*how she feels but*

*it's not quite right*

*and it leaves her cold...*

# Chapter60

*her eyes are neither*

*so fascinating nor attractive.*

*maybe it hold enough of*

*which neither seems*

*realistic nor imaginative.*

# Chapter 61

*her thoughts were destroying her.*

*she tried not to think*

*but the silence was a*

*KILLER too.*

# Chapter62

*she dares to stand still*

*amidst the CHAOS*

*which is silent.*

# Chapter 63

*SILENCE in SILENT*


*is a way much scary;*


*don't know what she is to*


*but she listens to it.*

# Chapter64

*sometimes it feels like*

*she is the book*

*with pages blank*

*and that she has to write*

*but is confused of the starting line.*

# Chapter65

*it seems like there will be rain;*

*there's a chance she can put off*

*her NaCl rolling down her cheeks*

*which is now erupting due to it's extremity.*

# Chapter66

*surpassing the days*

*in a hope of a magnificient morning*

*which normalizes the things*

*right back to its own reserved place.*

# Chapter67

*why the world seems*

*so cruel that you can't even exist ??*

*why the world seems*

*so very beautiful that you can't even exist ??*

*– an illusion*

# Chapter68

*she distance herself from*

*people*

*when she is not o'kay*

*because she didn't want to*

*be the source of*

*negativity.*

# Chapter69

she turns to be silent,


when a kind of war


of all those things


happens inside her brain.

# Chapter70

at times she is out of her,

she is out of this world.

maybe it can be a impact of the

fluctuations occured in her

neurons of the brain.

# Chapter71

*how interesting it would be ??*


*screaming instill silently...*

# Chapter72

*its not we who decide*

*when to feel what*

*- it just happens*

# Chapter 73

*sometimes it's better to*

*refer as we*

*than I.*

*– the click*

# Chapter74

*moonlight in the night*

*embraces her soul...*

*seeing the darkest side of her*

*the stars said:*

*'she has something in her forlorn.'*

# Chapter75

*toxic atmosphere moulds her into a piece,*


*where neither she can be happy nor sad,*


*neither she can run away nor she wants to stay.*


*- it's all time adventure for her*

# Chapter76

*above the clouds,*

*the crescent moon shines incandescently,*

*stars forming a constellation,*

*some brighter,*

*some lighter*

*and some in its lightest form*

*as if indicating a light of HOPE*

SUPRIYA SINGH

*in the darkest sky.*

*- darkest times*

# Chapter77

*she is a backslider*

*- a lost soul*

*to find what actually is lost*

*- herself or soul or*

*something which doesn't even exist*

# Chapter78

she wants to speak

but can't ,

she wants to live

but can't ,

to all those

she can't.

she just can't.

# Chapter 79

she goes on to mug up


of all that


into her brain


and then


it bursts out through her eyes.

# Chapter80

*seems like NIGHT*

*has the only power to*

*unleash her SOUL.*

# Chapter81

*from acting as though*

*moon is following us*

*then actually trying to*

*follow that moon*

*- somewhere the things and perspective got changed*

*with us.*

# Chapter82

somewhere she read;

'it's ordinary to love the beautiful,

but it's beautiful to love the ordinary.'

- it all got struck to her mind

# Chapter83

*you'll be*

*smiling through your*

***TEARS.***

# Chapter84

*she likes to be a mystery*

*and*

*she tries to just be that,*

*she literally tries...*

# Chapter85

*the moon is her*

*constant companion.*

*no complains,*

*no arguments.*

*– just listening her tales*

# Chapter86

she lies,

she lies to people,

she lies to her loved ones,

she lies to herself.

the things are better

than being at worst

because either she lies

*or she prefers to be silent.*

# Chapter87

*there's so much inside her*

*if it ever erupts*

*it will be nonethless*

*than a volcano erupting lava...*

# Chapter 88

*she does what she wants to,*

*whenever and wherever*

*she gets that opportunity...*

# Chapter89

*they asked:*

*'where she disappears all of a sudden at times?'*

*maybe she wanted to be with herself*

*with her own dilemmas*

*for that time being.*

# Chapter 90

*everything seems better*

*when*

*she's into books.*

# Chapter91

*she is not so full of angst*

*to prove herself right*

*when at times*

*she might be actually right.*

# Chapter 92

*she is a question mark;*

*about people,*

*about things,*

*about feelings,*

*about thoughts,*

*about HERSELF.*

# Chapter 93

*SHE THINKS TOO MUCH...*


*SHE FEELS TOO MUCH...*


*- it is a blunder*

# Chapter 94

she wants to run away from


all these chaos,


so far where no one knows her


but she can't


for the people


she can't leave them alone...

# Chapter95

*SHE*

*a great*

*PROCASTINATOR.*

# Chapter96

*family is good*

*unless it turns to be toxic*

*every second day...*

# Chapter97

*family problems and responsibilities*

*are so hard that*

*it takes away the person*

*and even his whole life at times.*

*- it sucks*

# Chapter98

*you need to be lucky*

*to have a suppotive family*

*and the one who*

*believes in you and your dreams...*

# Chapter99

*she is the child of*

*NATURE*

*nature nurtures HER...*

# Chapter100

*we are not aware to*

*how far our words*

*can impact someone...*

*so be cautious while throughing them out.*

# Chapter101

*she feels better to pen down*

*her feelings & thoughts*

*rather than*

*disclosing it to someone.*

# Chapter 102

*what about some friends*

*who make you feel devastated at times??*

*and they can't even feel that*

*on their own.*

# Chapter103

*it's all in the mind,*


*the people,*


*their words,*


*their actions,*


*it,s all there...*


*- they have their impact on her*

# Chapter 104

*right time,*

*what is the right time to be in love??*

# Chapter 105

*she just smiles*

*when they say:*

*'you seem so happy*

*with these little things'*

# Chapter106

love,


a mystery;


an unsolved mystery.


- for ages

# Chapter107

*love has the power*

*to let believe*

*even the impossible...*

# Chapter 108

under the moonlight,


fixing her glasses,


going through each verse and then verses;


the process continues and she is so indulged


in the world of her own that she forgets


she has to exist in another one.

# Chapter109

*it's hard to express*

*when*

*someone reads your eyes*

*and give remarks*

*which you were unable to speak out...*

*- all arenot efficient*

# Chapter110

*some stories are incomplete,*

*some stories are imperfect,*

*some of them have flaws too*

*but it doesn't mean*

*they are not beautiful.*

*- beautiful doesn't define a happy ending*

# Chapter111

*the darkness to be lit*

*in the shadow of*

**BELIEF.**

# Chapter112

*some desire to die*

*because death seems to be*

*the end of chaos,*

*end of pain*

*and end of oneself.*

# Chapter113

*it aches,*

*it pains,*

*it takes you over at times*

*when you are the reason of someone's sorrow,*

*when you are the reason of someone's pain,*

*knowingly or unknowingly;*

*intentionally or unintentionally,*

*doesn't matter much.*

# Chapter114

*at the end,*


*no one but one person*


*will be there for you.*


*you will be there for yourself,*


*only YOU.*

# Chapter 115

*life does to poets*

*what autumn does to trees.*

*we shed ourselves*

*naked on blanked pages as winds of words*

*carry us home.*

# Chapter 116

*feels like sinking,*

*and sinking,*

*and sinking;*

*it is dark,*

*it becomes darker*

*and darker.*

*- is it death*

# Chapter117

*at times,*

*parents don't realize*

*what their child can go through*

*and is going through.*

*they don't realize;*

*how matured they became before age*

*maybe because of them...*

*– maybe*

# Chapter118

her eyes were trying

it's best to hold those tears

when someone said:

'seems you are thinking something and

worried about it,

some days you are lost;

some or the other thing is constantly

*revolving in your brain*


*which you won't speak out.'*


*- she passed an unrealistic smile and said*


*nothing...*

# Chapter119

*she was in pain*

*so much that she can't even claim;*

*her mind aches,*

*her body aches*

*and*

*her heart aches*

*and*

*slowly soul drifts away...*

# Chapter 120

*heaven & hell,*

*a believer and a cynic,*

*love & hate,*

*life & death.*

*two contrasts of each other yet*

*when referred at times,*

*they are together.*

*then why not same in individuals??*

# Chapter121

*love is beautiful*

*in books,*

*in movies,*

*in dramas,*

*in life??*

# Chapter122

*with tears rolling down her cheeks*

*she sits alone gazing at the sky,*

*breeze passes through her skin*

*and the storm inside her arises...*

*tears are dried now,*

*wind passes through her skin,*

*the storm insider her is calm now...*

# Chapter123

*the observance is all you need,*

*you can find your answers*

*as do easily...*

# Chapter124

*an unkown and unidentified*

*reason is the reason*

*of her anti - social and melancholic*

*state of mind.*

# Chapter125

*white over blue,*

*pink slightly laping it,*

*grey was somewhere in mid,*

*black was covering it*

*as it was just looking like ...*

*- the sky*

# Chapter126

she is overjoyful,


she is overmatured,


she is overcheerful,


she is overthinker,


she is oversensitive,


she is overdepressed


and at the edge,

*she is OVER.*

# Chapter127

she's happy when the sunset is

ever beautiful to witness,

it feels good to just pass the time

gazing at the sky but don't know

why there is something special about night.

it sounds good to listen to the chirpings of birds

early morning,

*feels like actually nature has it's song too.*

*the aroma by still steaming tea and*

*she with her all coziness holding the*

*compilation of Gulzar's ghazals*

*as if like diving in the ocean full of corals...*

# Chapter128

*the night was beautiful,*

*stars emerged*

*and the moon too;*

*she feels like flying on that drive...*

*- she was living at that time*

# Chapter129

*sitting all alone,*

*she turns to be productive;*

*wondering at the skies at high*

*and plains at low,*

*the cool breeze passing through her soul,*

*she tries to find the words which can*

*describe hr forlorn;*

*puzzled somewhere mid*


*she tries to unfold...*

# Chapter130

*she learns secretly*

*knowingly,*

*unknowingly,*

*how to go with different people*

*at same time.*

*- genes*

# Chapter131

*what's the definition of beautiful ??*


*is there any definition of beautiful ??*

# Chapter132

*the star in north is said to be guiding*

*the sailors all through their journey*

*not to be misguided.*

*seeing it; felt it's quiet alone in that limitless sky,*

*shining a little bright devoiding it's own lightness;*

*regulating alone in that midpath.*

# Chapter133

*it's not easy at all*


*to admire sunrise and sunset*


*as well being in love with the moon and stars;*


*it's not easy at all...*

# Chapter134

*words are the sharpest weapon to kill anyone.*


*words are the lightest healer to heal anyone.*



*- life is a wordgame of living & dying*

# Chapter135

state of mind carved out on page,

dragging the nib throughout the lines;

showcasing it then whenever

they say:

' it's great.'

# Chapter136

*by losing yourself*

*what have you found for yourself ??*

# Chapter137

*moonlight beamed in the pink sky,*

*a tiny dot around was shining little bright,*

*carving out some creatures made of clouds;*

*she was sitting wandering*

*Is this also a way to howl ??*

*plugging in the headset, she goes into tune*

*and then after everyone seems to be mute.*

# Chapter138

*what hurts the most ??*

*...*

*...*

*...*

*everyone in this universe owns his.*

# Chapter139

*she is a dark.*

*she has a dark mind.*

*she has a dark soul.*

*she has a dark heart.*

*she is in dark.*

*she is a dark.*

# Chapter140

*wherever you are, at any moment,*

*try and find something beautiful.*

*a face, a line out of a poem,*

*the clouds out of a window, skies,*

*some graffiti, birds aligning on a wire,*

*sunset, a farm, a flower and so on...*

*beauty cleans the mind.*

# Chapter141

*3:10 a.m.*

*she woke up,*

*goes up the terrace,*

*she plugs in the headset,*

*played her playlist*

*and watches the moon & night.*

*she felt like 15 minutes but*

*actually it was 1 hour 40 minutes.*

# Chapter 142

Pain.

*she is in pain.*

*it didn't hurt her,*

*it's just the another one.*

*it's just that*

*she is in pain*

*and once again*

*no one knows that.*

# Chapter143

*sometimes you have to distance*

*yourself*

*so that if you meet next time,*

*it will be forever...*

# Chapter 144

*there's a moment when*

*sunrise and sunset*

*looks alike,*

*so does in people.*

# Chapter145

*A heart*


*- cause of everything.*

# Chapter146

is it necessary ??

to develop new things by destroying the old one ??

can't we keep the old one

maybe it's more beautiful

and take a while to process out the new one;

is it necessary ??

to destroy the old one in the making of new ??

# Chapter 147

*you are the best person ever*


*– when you are dead.*

# Chapter 148

*she is too matured of her age;*

*it's both,*

*a blessing and*

*a curse.*

# Chapter 149

she wrote her heart out


on the pages by hunting the words.


and every time it rained,


a new cloud of emotions was formed...

# Chapter150

*MOVE ON ;*

*these two words takes away a lot*

*from individuals...*

*and at times an individual...*

# Chapter151

*9:30 a.m.*

*it's a sunday morning,*

*she sits in a sunlight*

*with her cup and*

*a few more cups.*

*scorching heat darkens her skin*

*and she feels cold within...*

# Chapter152

*no one is going to be for you;*

*you have to fight for yourself,*

*you have to learn for yourself,*

*you have to grow for yourself,*

*you have to voice for yourself.*

# Chapter 153

*stary nights,*

*city lights,*

*busy people,*

*crowded places,*

*reckless sounds;*

*it's a life.*

# Chapter154

*life is very unpredicted;*

*at times,*

*you don't know which will be your*

*last goodbye to someone*

*or*

*whose goodbye will become last of theirs*

*to you.*

# Chapter155

*think twice;*

*before you speak*

*because you don't know*

*either it will be time or person*

*who will be standing against you*

*at that moment.*

# Chapter156

*it's not easy*

*to BELIEVE ;*

*it's not easy at all*

*to BELIEVE in*

*yourself.*

# Chapter157

*responsibilities weighs more*

*than dreams;*

*as you can see*

*as well as witness it*

*RESPONSIBILITIES takes over*

*DREAMS;*

*at times.*

# Chapter158

*friends are the reason*

*you feel happy,*

*friends are the reason*

*you smile,*

*friends are the reason*

*your day becomes better*

*and at times;*

*friends are the reason*

*of your sorrow,*

*friends are the reason*

*of your tears,*

*friends are the reason*

*your day becomes bitter.*

*– it switches*

# Chapter159

*the thoughts which are struck into mind,*

*the tears held into eyes;*

*I can't bear it now*

*somewhere it pulls me down*

*to be nowhere on mine.*

# Chapter 160

*emotions are delivered at wrong times;*

*sometimes*

*and this is where,*

*the probability of things and people*

*being messed up increases...*

# Chapter161

*REGRET*,

*GUILT*,

*SELF - DOUBT*,

*are the termites*

*which hollows an individual.*

# Chapter162

*she swims,*

*she is swimming,*

*she will swim*

*unless she reaches*

*her shore...*

# Dear Readers

*And here come to the end of chain of random thoughts and feelings which resides in a teenager. Thank you for bestowing your time and going through these few lines which are the consequent of puzzles, chaos and questions in one's head.*

*To all the readers who ever come across this, if you ever relate any one of them than I will consider myself to one of those who really knows people and can connect with them by words.*

*IT WILL BE GREATLY APPRECIATED IN SPREADING THESE WORDS BY YOU.*

*THANK YOU,*

*MY DEAR READER.*

# About The Author

*A teenager and a student of Convent School, Supriya Singh lives in her town Ballia, a district in Uttar Pradesh which has it's own history and holds a significant role in the freedom struggle of India. She is all set to complete her schooling from Holy Cross School, Amritpali, Ballia with commerce stream and is looking forward to pursue her graduation in the same field.*

*She loves to play with words and synchronise them in a manner to express herself. She started to express her thoughts by reflecting it on pages when she was fourteen and gradually developed an interest in carving out her own niche down the pages and has become a part of her life which she would like to take forward throughout her life.*

*She believes this world is abundant of beautiful storieswhich are unsaid and undiscovered. Everyone in this universe has it's own story; they just need to find their way of expressing theirs and this world will be full of stories, artists and art which will turn this world into a really beautiful one.*

• 186 •

*You can contact her at (singhsupriya2910@gmail.com) .*

# Acknowledgements

*THANK YOU.*

*To my parents.*

*To everyone who jogged my memory and who contributed their part to my life.*

*To people who have been a support system in this and who have been constantly assuring me that it will be a better one when questions arose about it in my head,now and then. All I have to do is to give time and believe in the process.*

*To the team at Notion Press who has constantly supported and guided along the process and had been patiently waiting for the outcome.*